Walks in TOTNES Countryside

Bob Mann

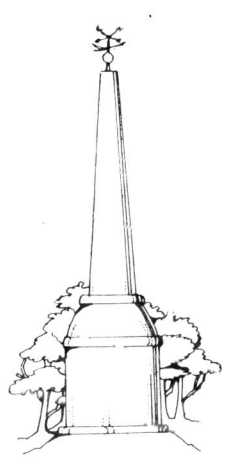

OBELISK PUBLICATIONS

ALSO BY THE AUTHOR
Boat Trip Down the Dart
The Ghosts of Totnes
Buckfast and Buckfastleigh
SOME OTHER TITLES FROM OBELISK
The Great Little Totnes Book, *Chips Barber*
The Totnes Collection, *Bill Bennett*
Diary of a Dartmoor Walker, *Chips Barber*
Diary of a Devonshire Walker, *Chips Barber*
Ten Family Walks on Dartmoor, *Sally and Chips Barber*
Ten Family Walks in East Devon, *Sally and Chips Barber*
Walks in the South Hams, *Brian Carter*
Pub Walks in the South Hams, *Brian Carter*
Walks in the Shadow of Dartmoor, *Denis McCallum*
Walks in Tamar and Tavy Country, *Denis McCallum*
Wheelchair Walks in Devon, *Lucinda Ruth Gardner*
The Great Walks of Dartmoor, *Terry Bound*
For further details of these or any of our titles, please send an SAE to Obelisk Publications at the address below, or telephone (01392) 468556

Acknowledgments

Many thanks first of all to Ffyona Campbell, the courageous and determined young woman who walked around the world between 1984 and 1994, and who was born in Totnes, for her generous foreword. Also to: Maya Hussell, the companion for most of my way; my mother, Ellen Mann, who first took me walking in the country around Totnes; Sally and Chips Barber; Valerie Belsey for highway history; Janet, Christine and Samm at the Totnes Tourist Information Centre for constant help; Trevor Drew, editor of the *Totnes Times*, in which much of this book first appeared in slightly different form; and finally to my fellow writers and editors on the *U.K. Express* for continual inspiration and stimulation.

Plate Acknowledgements
All maps by Sally Barber
All photographs by or belonging to Chips Barber

This book is dedicated to all who walk in and appreciate the landscapes of South Devon.

First published in 1995 by
Obelisk Publications, 2 Church Hill, Pinhoe, Exeter, Devon
Designed by Chips and Sally Barber
Typeset by Sally Barber
Printed in Great Britain by
The Devonshire Press Limited, Torquay, Devon

© **Bob Mann/Obelisk Publications 1995**

All Rights Reserved. No part of this publication may be reproduced, stored in a retrieval system, or transmitted, in any form or by any means, electronic, mechanical, photocopying, recording or otherwise, without the prior permission of the publishers and copyright holders.

Walks in the TOTNES Countryside

**Foreword
by Ffyona Campbell**

Bob Mann has written a practical yet beautifully descriptive guide to walks in the Totnes area. So full of folklore treasures and natural history observations, I felt as though I'd done the walks myself without having to don the boots. A wonderful book for both avid walker and curious armchair explorer.

River Dart

Introduction

The lovely and historic South Devon town of Totnes is built, as are so many ancient towns and cities, on a hill above a bend in a tidal estuary, in this case that of the River Dart, and seems to grow naturally out of the rich landscape surrounding it. Having been born in the town and lived most of my life in or near it, I cannot remember a time when I did not know intimately the country stretching away in every direction, and walking through it has been an enduring pleasure. Within easy reach of the centre there is a wide range of terrains to enjoy: fields and woods, hills, watermeadows and wetlands, above all the network of green lanes leading out of Totnes and taking you almost immediately into what appear to be the depths of the South Hams countryside. This book is a celebration of some of these walks which, I hope, will encourage both locals and visitors to discover the pleasure and interest, even romance, that can be gained from familiarity with them. There is enough variety and beauty to last several lifetimes.

Much of the book is based on material from my 'Mann About Town' column in the *Totnes Times* over the last few years, the main theme of which has been the importance of valuing and understanding the special qualities and characteristics of wherever we are: what used to be called the genius *loci*, and now tends to be described as 'local distinctiveness.' Walking around a place is the most satisfying way of getting to know it, and at a time when change is so constant, dramatic and seemingly chaotic, people need more than ever to appreciate the particular locations in which they find themselves. If we can feel connected to a place, involved in its life, knowing its stories, its landscapes and wildlife, the layer upon layer of human experience behind it, then we shall naturally acquire the wisdom to know what kind of change and development is appropriate and what isn't. This can be equally the case whether we are indigenous locals, exogenous settlers or simply staying a while to study and explore.

Dartington

Casual visitors can also experience this connection, and in fact it seems to be a part of Devon's appeal as a holiday resort to give people a sense of rootedness; even if they have only just arrived, they feel as if they have been here for ever. In a place so beautiful and resonant, of course, it is not difficult to care about the quality of the environment. What is harder is for us to have this sense of responsibility and understanding for the whole planet, wherever our place on it happens to be.

However, this book is not another polemic on the importance of good ecology; it is simply an expression of the enjoyment I have had and continue to have in wandering around my native territory, from which I have never felt any great desire to move, being happy to remain enfolded by the rounded hills and deep lanes of the Dart Valley. In this I am the opposite of my fellow Totnesian Ffyona Campbell, but even with her great achievement of walking around the world, I am sure she would find places in the area of her home town as satisfying to explore as anywhere more exotic (and, considering the erratic way some of the local lanes are signposted, possibly as challenging!).

These walks, then, are a celebration of Totnes and its surrounding country, and the qualities which make it special. Other landscapes may be more mysterious or dramatic – Cornwall, parts of Dorset and the Somerset levels are obvious examples in the South West – and some are equally beautiful, but this part of South Devon, between Dartmoor and the sea, seems to possess an intensity, almost visionary at times, which can be felt nowhere else, deriving perhaps from the constant rising and falling of the hills, the lushness of growth and, more than anything, the contrast between red soil, green foliage and the blue of sea and sky, which can be so startling that when painting the landscape it is usually necessary to tone them down, for fear of making them unbelievable.

My own feeling of rootedness in this place is certainly deepened by walking around it, as much as by writing about its history, folklore and creative associations, but awareness of these also feeds my pleasure in the walks. My appreciation of a landscape is enhanced by knowing what others have felt and written about it. There is a strange satisfaction in knowing that where I walk today other people once walked, and left their impressions for me to enjoy. The nineteenth century Totnes naturalist Francis George Heath, for example, described in detail many of the lanes around the town, some of which have not changed in over a hundred years. The works of contemporary Devon authors like Brian Carter, Anne Born and Samantha Benedikte, whose *Rainsongs and River Music* is a constant companion, also add to the richness of my walking experience, creating, with my own memories, ever more layers of meaning and pleasure. Generations of English writers have, after all, celebrated the joys of stepping out on the road or into the country, and I often wonder what Hazlitt, Chesterton or John Cowper Powys would have made of the Totnes area. Going for a walk thus becomes an adventure of the imagination, even of the spirit. For many people an intimate knowledge of the flora and fauna does the same thing.

Inevitably all my journeys, local or distant, must start from this steep, grey-

roofed little town beside the Dart, but it also feels a good place in which to finish a journey, however far away it began. Walking into Totnes from the country, especially the heights to the south and east, from Kingsbridge Hill or Totnes Down Hill, seeing the whole of it stretched out below, backed by the woods of Dartington and the patchwork of green and red fields, with Dartmoor in the distance, you feel a natural sense of homecoming. You make your way into town through narrow roads lined with old walls covered in moss, lichens, ferns and valerian, and past comfortable, spacious houses. The great Irish playwright Sean O'Casey, who lived here from 1938 to 1955, described Totnes as looking like an old 'grey-haired lady, with a young face, sitting calm, hands in lap, unmindful of time, in an orchard of ageing trees, drowsy with the scent of ripened apples about to fall, but which never do...' A touch whimsical, but from here you can understand just what he meant.

Or, coming from Torbay, at the top of Bridgetown Hill, you look down the main road winding past the neat walls and trees which hide the Edwardian villas, and see the original hilltop town with its church and castle, compact and perfect. The Victorian poet and theologian John Keble sat here and wrote a poem about the view below him, invoking the 'feudal towers' and 'happy valley', and considering the 'flowers of peace and home' which could grow here. He was right, and despite the ubiquitous pressures and confusions of the late twentieth century, a good life can still be lived in Totnes.

It will be clear that this is not one of those walking books which merely gives curt instructions on where to go and what to wear! Distilled from over thirty years of wandering about the area, at all seasons, it is a frankly personal response to its beauties and stories. Nevertheless, I hope the routes can be easily followed, and that the factual information is accurate and useful. Distances and times are very approximate, as, because of the hills, a walk can seem a lot longer than it really is. All the walks are described as beginning from the Tourist Information Centre on the Plains, at the bottom of the town, where the staff are always immensely helpful and where you can buy a fine selection of books and maps (you are not venturing where there is much danger of getting lost, but maps are always useful as well as fascinating, and the one you need is the Ordnance Survey 'Landranger'

one-and-a-quarter inch Torbay and South Dartmoor sheet 202). Likewise, each walk returns to the town, where, according to taste and the time of day, you can seek refreshment in one of the many cafes, pubs or wine bars. As for what to wear, including footwear, choose whatever you will be comfortable in, bearing in mind that the lanes are liberally endowed with brambles, nettles and sharp branches, and even in the summer are likely to be muddy. A quality of the red Devon soil is that once it gets onto your clothes it is there for ever, reminding you always of your adventures in field and footpath.

So gather together all that you want to take – food and drink, binoculars, sketch pad, bird books, flower books or whatever will enhance the journey for you, without weighing yourself down too much – and set off into the Totnes countryside for what will doubtless be a series of memorable rambles through some of the best landscapes in South Devon, which you will recall with pleasure for years to come.

— WALK ONE —
THROUGH FIELDS, WOODS AND WETLANDS TO ASHPRINGTON AND BACK

This is possibly the most challenging walk in the book, and perhaps not for the frail or fainthearted, but the effort is rewarded by the chance to get intimately close to some unforgettable country, and you will feel very virtuous by the end. Approx. four and a half miles, taking about two and a half hours.

From the Tourist Information Centre turn right and walk along by the river past the new houses towards the Steam Packet Inn. This area has changed greatly over the centuries: originally marsh, it was reclaimed about two hundred years ago and made into a tree-lined pleasure ground with a bowling green. In the late nineteenth century it became an industrial quay, complete with a railway line to the station, where timber, cement and other commodities were imported, and the once famous Totnes cider taken away. Wooden minesweepers were built here during the Second World War. In front of the Steam Packet car park is a low wall and a very faded plaque; all that is left of the Taunton Monument or 'castle and keys', an entertaining folly built in 1825 to represent the town coat of arms, an archway flanked by towers and two keys. Unfortunately it fell into neglect and was demolished by a timber lorry in 1957, but judging from old postcards and paintings, it was very atmospheric indeed. William Doidge Taunton was mayor of Totnes in 1824.

Just behind the pub a sign directs you to the footpath through a yard, and soon

you climb over a stile into some fields, with what survives of Totnes's timber trade, carried on these days by road rather than river, below you on the left. Across the river is a path along what is known as the Longmarsh, an area much loved by the people of Totnes, and the subject of a later walk. The fields above you on the brooding hillside are steep, springy and often damp; there is a stream where, when very young, I picked watercress. Bracken grows higher up, and at the end of the timberyard you climb towards some dark woods. Look back for a classic view of the town on its hill, rising out of the river, with castle and church tower standing out against the sky and Hay Tor in the distance, then enter the wood through the new gateway. Until recently this section of the walk could only be done at low tide, as you had to go down onto the beach; now a new path takes you through the trees. In a few years the track will look as if it has been here for ever. Listen for the distinctive cry of a woodpecker; I have associated the sound with these woods since my earliest childhood, and the walk never feels complete without it.

Emerging into another steep field, with the beautifully rounded hills across the river, you feel you are already deep in the country. Opposite, two hundred feet up, is the compelling ruin of Windwhistle Cottage, and at the end of the field you

reach World's End, the site of a long-vanished farm. The low walls which remain are all that is left of the first Totnes sewage works, in use until a few years ago. Don't go forward into the wetland though, but follow the edge of the fields where the solid hillside suddenly meets the marshes, a powerful and fascinating juxtaposition. If in doubt about the route, look for the yellow Devon County Council footpath markers.

This is a walk for quick, intense impressions of the sort of landscapes the Dart

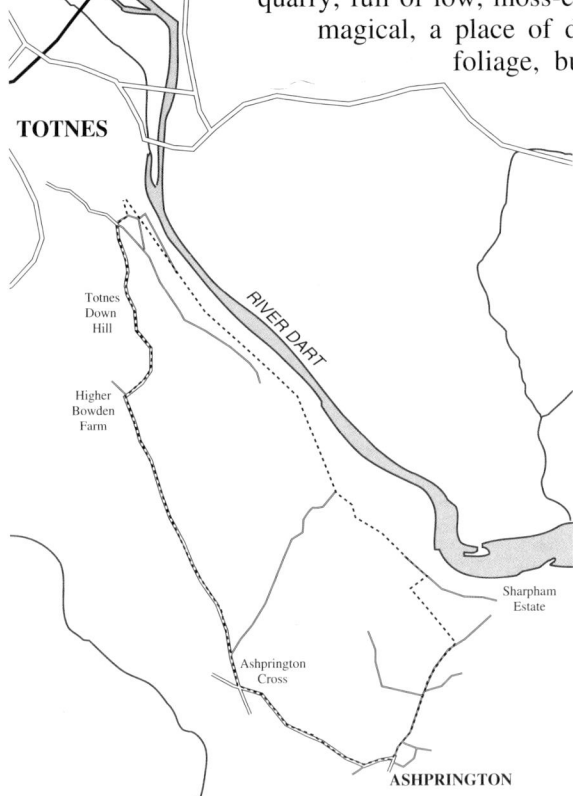

Valley can provide. Barely have you left the woods than you find yourself in a swampy morass, actually a disused quarry, full of low, moss-covered trees. It can be quite magical, a place of dark pools and bright green foliage, but it is not always easy to negotiate, and mind the barbed wire. Soon a stile brings you to another field. Keep to the edge of this. Windwhistle stands out dramatically on its hill opposite, with buzzards very often circling above and sheep moving mysteriously upon the slope. Beside you the reeds of the wide saltmarshes give shelter to shelduck, reed warblers, sedge warblers, sandpipers and curlew. Now you cross another stile into a newly planted field of broadleaved trees, which will one day be a pleasant copse of sycamore, beech, birch, wild cherry and American red oak. Leaving this you enter a large, steeply ridged field with a stream running down across it. After such an intense section of the walk, this is a good place for a rest, as you still have quite a bit of climbing to do. You can either remain close to the bottom of the field or strike up towards the plantation, where a muddy track skirts the low, mossy wall.

Keep on towards the left, and soon you will reach two gates and a bridge over a stream. The footpath joins for a while the drive leading to Sharpham, but then turns right, straight up the steepest hill you have yet had to climb. Walk backwards – not only is it good for the thigh muscles, it also gives you the most beautiful and satisfying views back up the river valley towards Totnes, and down the estuary, with all that fertile country round about. It may be childish, but this walk invariably makes me think of the 'Wayfarers All' chapter in *The Wind in the Willows*. I suppose it is a sense of the estuary winding away, past fields and high woods, out of the secure home landscape towards distant travel and adventure. At the top of the slope you enter some more woods and continue along the track between the trees, with the river shining below, until the track becomes a lane. In spring the woods are rich in bluebells and other flowers, but you may have other things to concentrate on: this is often the muddiest part of a walk already quite rich in mud.

Coming out on to the metalled road you see on the left two pillars marking the entrance to the Sharpham Estate, now known for its wine and cheese and as a venue for talks, workshops and retreats of a spiritual nature. Walk on towards the village of Ashprington, however, which soon appears, all pretty cottages, well-kept gardens, grey, lichened walls and a feeling of gentility and peace. The rich plateau of the South Hams is laid out below.

Passing the little grey church of St David, an unusual dedication in this part of the world and suggestive of Celtic origins, turn right in the centre of the village and onto the road towards Totnes. Lovely countryside is glimpsed through gateways and over hedges, and Dartmoor soon appears on the skyline. Turn right at the crossroads. This is one of my favourite roads, with wonderful views on the right, taking in once again the river with its wetlands, and the hills rising and

falling towards Torbay and the sea. When walking along it in the opposite direction I always have a strong sense of the 'Wayfarers All' atmosphere: the feeling of setting off on the winding road towards romance and discovery, even if my destination is only one of the many enjoyable pubs that can be reached by it. I never tire of the contrast in this area between the red of the soil and the green of the grass, and the ploughed fields sometimes glow as if lit from within. It is high up and this road can be windy – the effect of the 1990 storms is still apparent in the woods – but the hedges are strong and sheltering, and I have seen primroses along here in December.

At Higher Bowden Farm the road turns right onto Totnes Down Hill, and soon the grey, white and red buildings of the town are below, with a fair amount of fair Devonshire visible around it. The road winds down between banks of fern, and is narrow, so that you frequently have to fall back into the hedge to allow cars to pass. Soon you are at Cherry Cross, a restored medieval monument by the side of the road, and turning right down Moat Hill you easily find your way back to where you started the walk.

— WALK TWO —
HARPER'S HILL, JACKMAN'S LANE AND COPLAND LANE

A rocky ramble along some of the steepest lanes around Totnes, with expansive views over South Devon. Approx. three miles, taking two hours.

Leaving the information office, turn left and make your way up the main street of the town, enjoying its varied but somehow unified architectural styles. If it is a Friday, stop to look at the market below the Civic Hall, where you can buy anything from incense holders to didgeridoos, cat food to biodynamically grown vegetables, and experience the colourful and diverse culture of contemporary Totnes. The Friday market is indeed a wonderful place, where the conventional small town and the 'New Age capital' come together against the backdrop of old houses and the beautiful river valley stretching away between green hills, and where you can see jugglers, buskers, healers, astrologers, mystics, ageing hippies, farmers, counsellors, councillors, the brilliant, the wild, the lovely, the mad, as well as perfectly ordinary, well-balanced people like yourself.

But tear yourself away after a while and continue up the street, crossing the main road

at the top and continuing upwards, on what soon becomes a rocky, muddy country lane. It is an extraordinary and sudden change, but it must have been even more remarkable before the main road was built in the 1930s, and the street just became a lane without any warning. This is Harper's Hill, which climbs Windmill Down, and during the Middle Ages there was a well, Harper's Well, that supplied much of the town's water: it just came off the hill and ran down the

street. The lane is also known to locals as the Roman Road, but there is no historical evidence that it was one. Visitors to the town asking for the Harper's Hill Mushroom Farm are often bemused when locals tell them it is 'up the Roman Road'. There was a windmill on Windmill Down from the fourteenth century, but no trace of it remains.

Being a natural romantic, autumn is my favourite time for revisiting old haunts, and the first time I walked up here for several years was one day in October, when the colours were as rich as the memories the walk brought back. I lived at the top of this lane for an autumn, some years ago, in a caravan, and I thought of the people I used to know at the nearby farm. We would make our way down the hillside on Friday nights for a drink in the town, and in the dark, or in bad weather, it was a major expedition: I always felt that we had earned our drink much more than if we lived opposite the pub and just had to step across the road. I thought too of an artist friend who once lived up here, David Shanahan, 'Shan' as he signs himself, who is the only person I know who can get away with painting the colours of the Devon landscape in all their vividness and intensity.

On this October day the leaves were many shades of red and brown, but the ferns below them in the bank were still green and fresh. The path is stony and sometimes difficult, but after a while it evens out a bit and runs straight between high hedgebanks. It is an unforgettable experience to walk up here in the rain, when the path is literally a series of waterfalls, and the sound of water is all about you. This was a major Devon highway for centuries, and shows what all the roads in the county must have been like before the days of the turnpikes. Charles I and his army passed along here during the Civil War, and for over a thousand years travellers of all kinds, tinkers, merchants, soldiers, minstrels, vagabonds, holy men, seamen and countless others must have journeyed where you now walk. Put them all together in your imagination and send them to Totnes market...

Stop at a gateway on the right for panoramic views over the rich landscape towards Dartmoor, with the network of fields and woods, the occasional church tower, the white and grey farms and houses between the trees. I always get a feeling, walking through this countryside, that the people in these scattered homes must all be leading rich, creative, satisfying, exciting lives; no doubt, being human, many of them are leading cross, miserable and frustrated lives as well, but it is difficult not to feel a sense of wellbeing and spaciousness at the thought of living in such an environment.

High up on the left is Windmill Down Farm. Climb the steps in the bank for a moment just to look back and marvel at the view. This hill is undoubtedly a magical place, where it feels natural to come in search of inspiration and insight, or just to absorb the peace and beauty of the surrounding country.

Past the farm you soon come out on to the road to Harberton and Sandwell. Turning right, walk for about half a mile along what feels like an ancient ridgeway. Watch for buzzards wheeling above the fields. Soon another green lane appears on the right, running steeply downhill. This is Jackman's Lane, and again it is lush with ferns and growth of all kinds. On the right is an old reservoir, one of many on the heights around Totnes.

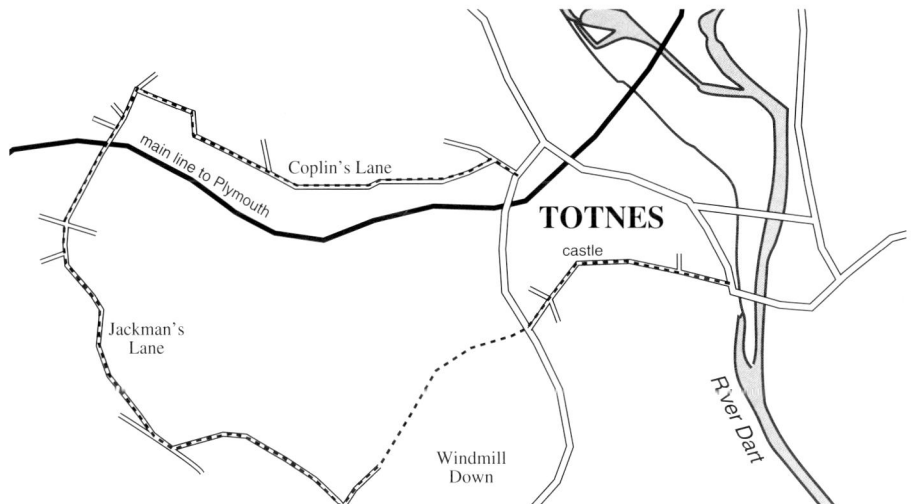

At the bottom of the lane you find yourself on the higher Plymouth road, at the very outskirts of the town, and the only entrance to it where there is long ribbon development of houses and bungalows. Cross straight over, however, and walk down the shady lane towards Dartington, past the bright new Follaton estate and across the railway bridge. After a rather steep hill another lane entrance appears on the right: this is Copland or Coplin's lane, and will take you back to Totnes. It tends to be muddy, but is, at least at this end, rich in plant and bird life. When you reach a junction with another lane on the left, keep going straight on. Soon a large new housing development appears on your left. The people here are fortunate in having such a classic Devon lane at the end of their gardens, but it is a pity it is often so full of rubbish and dog droppings. Never mind; after such an uplifting and invigorating walk you don't want to let anything lower your enjoyment. You soon leave the lane at the bottom of Barracks Hill, and cross the main road for the town.

— WALK THREE —
ALONG THE RIVER TO DARTINGTON AND BACK

A fairly easy walk embracing footpaths, an ancient estate, up-market shops and dreams of utopia. About three and a half miles, taking one and a half to two hours, depending on how long you linger.

Cross from the Plains to the left side of the bridge as if going over to Bridgetown, but take the steps down to the Riverside Path (at unusually high

tides this is not possible; instead go to the railway station and follow signs for the cycle path). It is good to be suddenly so close to the river, and I have always loved the way the garage buildings on the left come out over the water. Ducks and swans nest on the rough banks – I have watched a swan on her nest only yards from the footpath.

Go on past the superstore and under the new bridge. This walk is a constant feast to the senses, with all the sounds and smells of the river on one side, and those of the industrial estate on the other. Originally the whole of this area was tidal marsh, and looking back at the town above you, it is easy to appreciate the defensive strength of its natural site. Up until the Second World War this was Totnes Racecourse. The route involved two crossings of the river, which must have been rough for the horses.

16 Walks in the Totnes Countryside

The path follows the river around to the right, past the sewage works, where the little river Hems joins the Dart, and goes pleasantly along beneath the trees. Cormorants can often be seen fishing in the river, and it is always worth looking out for kingfishers. Himalayan balsam, with its erotically exploding seedpods, grows by the bank; hold the pod gently until it bursts open. As you get to the railway bridge another path from the station joins this one, and this is where you cross for the steam railway to Buckfastleigh. Continuing on you can hear the weir, and a wooden bridge takes you over the narrow leat to the college playing field. Turn right: you are now on the Totnes to Dartington Cycle Path, so look out for cyclists.

Just past the weir the river is still and inviting; generations of Totnes children learnt to swim here before the pool was built in the Borough Park. A couple of stone stiles can be seen by the path, and on the right the muddy little Bidwell Brook flows sluggishly into the Dart, in an area abundant with wetland plants.

Now you come out onto a metalled road and turn right through the lodge gates into the Dartington estate, walking along by flat watermeadows, which are prone to flooding, hanging woods and a line of mature oaks by the road which the pavement runs around. Keep following the drive as it goes up and down beside the river, with expansive views across to Torbay, not forgetting to look back at Totnes, nestling securely below the hills.

At the bottom of a slope a gate leads into the lower part of Dartington gardens, but keep on the drive and go up towards the buildings, then enter the gardens on the path with the cattle grid. Ahead of you is the Great Hall of Dartington, originally built in the fourteenth century by John Holand, Duke of Exeter and half-brother of Richard II, but the estate goes back to Saxon times. In more recent centuries it was owned by the Champernownes, one of Devon's leading families.

In 1925 Dartington was discovered by a Yorkshire gentleman called Leonard Elmhirst, who decided it was the perfect place for the 'experiment' he and his wife-to-be, Dorothy, an American heiress, planned for the regeneration of rural life. Their vision was complex and diverse, and they never liked to define it too clearly, but their aim was to show that a full, creative and economically viable life could be lived in a rural community, a noble intention at a time of great agricultural depression and poverty. They founded an avant garde coeducational boarding school, promoted modern methods of farming and forestry, encouraged the crafts and small business, and patronised the arts on a grand scale. It was a confusing, idealistic, progressive, internationalist, modernist dream, expressed in the clear, functional lines of many of its buildings, as well as in the free and uninhibited lifestyles of some of its participants, among them a few of the great names of the twentieth century – all improbably set down in the ancient and conservative Devon countryside.

Seventy years later, Dartington is no longer the 'world apart' it often seemed in the past, and to most visitors it is just a high class arts and conference centre like many others, with perhaps lovelier grounds. But something of the original vision and idealism is still in the air as you walk around the hall and gardens; music flows out of open windows, beautiful students from the College of Arts wander or sit beneath the trees.

From the gate at the top of the gardens there is a magnificent view across to the moors. Turn left down the hill, with the great white pile of Foxhole, the 1930s progressive school, ahead of you. On the left you pass High Cross House, which you will either love or loathe. Square, stark, bright blue, it was built by the American architect William Lescaze for Bill Curry, first headmaster of the school. It is now a museum displaying many of the modern artworks purchased by the Elmhirsts, a remarkable collection by any standards.

At the fork in the road turn left towards Foxhole, which now houses a host of small businesses, and go on past the cricket field. I caught sunstroke here at the age of five, having been brought by my parents to watch a match, and I haven't been able to appreciate cricket since.

At the bottom of the hill is the Dartington Cider Press Centre, a complex of

quality craft and gift shops with restaurant and gallery. Originally a farm, it became the home of Dartington's cider making business between the wars. It took on its present form in 1977, but I liked it just before that when there was an unpretentious, old-fashioned tea room here. Either stay to look around, or carry on past the wooden toy shop, built as a workshop for the potter Bernard Leach, and walk along by the river. You soon have a choice: the footpath on the left goes behind the watermill, the cycle path on the right goes in front of it. They meet again just past the entrance. The mill was built in the 1930s for the famous Dartington Hall Tweeds, and is now a printing works. Beyond it you are on the cycle path again. Keep going through the rather dark section past a woodyard, and you will soon be crossing the extensive water meadow on a pleasant, undulating track beneath the woods.

This was at one time a tidal creek of the River Dart, and it doesn't take much imagination to visualise it as it would have looked. After heavy rain you don't need any imagination, as it very easily floods, and large numbers of water birds can be seen on it, including flocks of geese. In spring, bluebells seem to cascade down the hillside on the left. After a while you come out again on the Dartington Hall Drive, and retrace your route back to the footbridge over the leat.

Here you can either return along the river walk to your starting place, or go along the cycle path to the railway station and into the town.

— WALK FOUR —
BRIDGETOWN, BOURTON AND BERRY POMEROY

Along roads and green lanes, through town and landscape rich in human and natural history. Approx. four miles, taking about one and a half hours.

Cross over the bridge and walk up through Bridgetown, taking a look at its many architectural styles. Until the great Reform Act of 1832 this was a separate borough from Totnes, and part of the parish of Berry Pomeroy. It was founded during the thirteenth century by the lords of the manor at Berry, who no doubt saw the value of a river port on their side of the Dart. It is first recorded as 'Brigg', but was later known as Bridgetown Pomeroy. It has some spacious houses and terraces of the eighteenth and early nineteenth centuries, but I especially like the older buildings around the Albert Inn, with their steep roofs and former shop windows. With seagulls wheeling overhead, you can easily see in your imagination the little medieval river town rising out of the marshes. In the mid-Victorian period there were six pubs between here and the Newton Abbot road.

Traditionally when the merchants and traders of Totnes reached a certain level of prosperity they moved from living over the shop out into the country. At the turn of the century they instead began to have their mansions built here, so we have the slopes of higher Bridgetown covered in tree-sheltered villas, like a slice of Torquay set down above the Dart. At this time the people of Totnes began to refer to the wealthy inhabitants of Bridgetown as 'Shark's Islanders.'

So make your way through Shark's Island, past the Newton Abbot turning and on up the hill. Opposite the redbrick shell of the old Cottage Hospital, now sadly boarded up, Bourton Road leads off to the left. Walk along here, past the entrance to Jubilee Road and over the hill. You are suddenly out of the suburbs and in the country, with a lovely expanse of variegated fields below you, rising gently upwards: a dream of red-soil Devon. Forget the pressures of your life as you walk down into it, by the grey stone buildings of what is very much a working farm, and up the lane, pausing to look back at the town, which always seems hazy from here: I have caught it looking almost as faint as a mirage on hot summer afternoons.

This lane is a good one for gnarled old trees, high hedgebanks full of ferns and flowers – especially violets – in the spring and summer, and ever-changing vistas of rounded hills. It has a strong sense of the traffic of past ages; this was the main road to Newton Abbot and Exeter until the present one was built in the early nineteenth century, and later on you will see what the rocky surface of a pre-Macadam highway was like. In *The Ghosts of Totnes* I described how many people feel that this lane is haunted, and although I have never experienced anything of a psychic nature here, it can have an atmosphere of mystery and stillness. Those who are sensitive can feel the presence, over to the right, of the haunted castle of Berry Pomeroy: invisible but not far away, 'standing quietly, an ancient castle embraced in the tranquil forest.'

The awareness of past ages is increased when, at the top of the hill, you come to two rounded stone gateways, covered in ivy, of which there is a lot in these lanes, and on the left is a restored well with a stone roof over it. In late summer the huge stalks of giant hogweed gone to seed add their decay to the sense of mystery. Perhaps the source of the 'feeling' of this lane is in the very ground itself; the rock changes just here from slate to limestone. A lane branches off to the right, but don't take it; you'll join up with it a bit later.

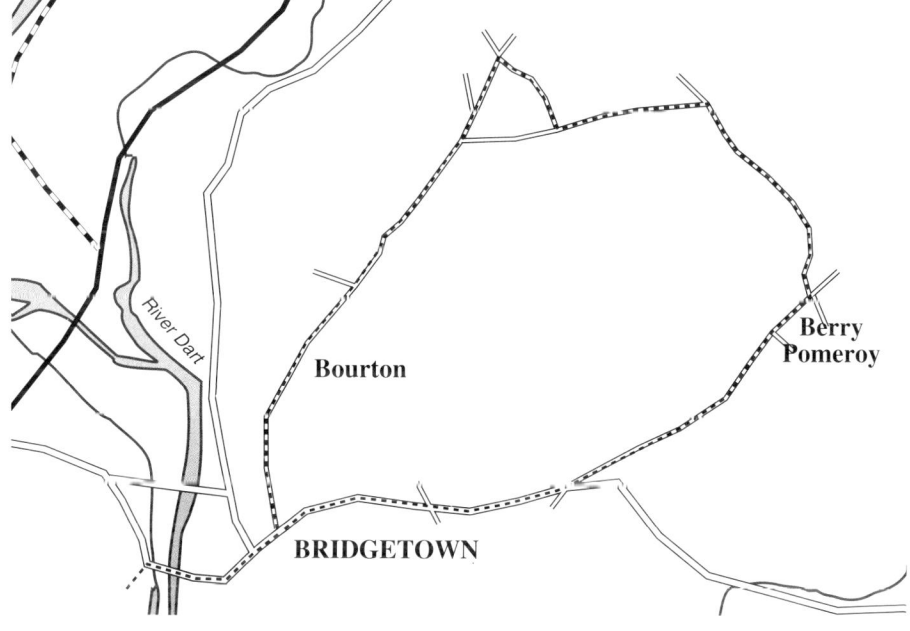

Walks in the Totnes Countryside

21

If you walk into it as far as the bent tree, however, you get a magnificent view back over the valley.

Continuing on, you come across the brow of the hill and reach another fork to the left; this leads down to the attractive village of Littlehempston. Continue to the right, stopping by the mossy wall to take in the wonderful sight of all that rich country, stretching between Dartmoor and Torbay, spread out in front of you. On a clear day Dartmoor looks close enough to step into.

The rocky path now reaches a crossroads, and so historic does it feel that you almost expect to meet a group of cloaked figures. The surface of the lane is probably no later than the sixteenth century. Take the right bend into an intimate little lane which in the autumn is abundant with blackberries. In the fields on the left are horses from the nearby stables, and behind them the dark spruce woods heighten the brightness of the hills. Soon you come out onto the lane you didn't take earlier, and turn left. This is an excellent place to find butterflies and dragonflies, but please do not indulge in the horrible old Devon tradition of killing the first butterfly of the year, if you should see it here (or anywhere else, for that matter!).

Soon the lane comes out on the road to Berry Pomeroy, with the ancient walls of the manorial deer-park crossing the field in front of you; the old ivy-covered stones, with rooks flying around them and moving about the field, can be a dramatic sight. Turn right towards the tiny village, with its grey cottages and orchards, sitting contentedly below the clump on Windmill Hill and with the

solid tower of St Mary's church rising above the trees. If you have time, pay a visit to the church, with its extravagant monument to the Seymour family, and meditate on the peaceful life of John Prince, vicar of the parish and author of a book which has been cherished for centuries by students of Devon history: *Worthies of Devon*.

Prince (1643-1723) was born near Axminster, and was vicar of Totnes until, in 1681, the Seymours offered him the living here; he took it, and remained until his death, improving the fabric of the church, seeing the last great days of the castle and working on his book. This is a voluble and colourful celebration of his native county and the great men it has produced. His aim was to uplift and inspire; he 'delighted not in that stinking employment of weeding men's lives, and throwing the nauseous trash upon their tombs' (what he would say about the art of biography today doesn't bear thinking about). 'Devon', he proclaims, was formerly 'rough and woody, hilly and mountainous, wild and rocky. But now, by the matchless labour and industry of its inhabitants, it yields a great abundance of all things which the earth, air and water can afford for the use of man.' Looking around at the fertile country in which he spent over forty years of his life, his complacence is understandable.

The road from Berry Pomeroy to Totnes is busy, but there is a pavement beside it, sometimes one side, sometimes the other. At True Street (in 1268 it was 'Trustede' – a place marked by a tree) it joins the main road from Paignton, which is even busier. The footpath continues along on the right, however, and you can ignore the noise and fumes beside you by looking once more down at the valley across which you have walked, until you reach the top of Bridgetown. From here you make your way through its genteel purlieus to the bridge and back to your starting place.

Walks in the Totnes Countryside

— WALK FIVE —
DOWN ALONG THE LONGMARSH

An easy but refreshing stroll by the River Dart, about two miles and taking an hour or less.

Leave the Plains and cross over into Bridgetown, turning right just after the bridge into Seymour Road, then right again into Steamer Quay Road, shady with horse-chestnuts. Soon you reach Steamer Quay, busy in the summer with the river-boats to Dartmouth, and touts from the rival companies anxious to sell you a ticket, but I like it in the autumn and winter as well, when all is closed up and pleasantly nostalgic, all greys and browns, with the river running fast and choppy and mist hanging over the hills.

Walk along by the river, through the car park and past the various industrial buildings. Ahead of you, at the end of the timber yard on the opposite bank, you can see the steep wooded hillside sloping right down to the water: a sign that you will soon be away from the town and its activity. Although the timber yard – known as Baltic Wharf – is still operating, it is several years since any ships from Scandinavia unloaded here, but they were familiar visitors in the 1960s and 70s.

Our destination is the Longmarsh, an area of about twelve acres originally reclaimed from the river during the nineteenth century, and a place where generations of townspeople have walked, played and courted. It was a very special place for me as a child: it began with an exciting area of long grass, trees and bushes, since buried beneath the Rowing Club and the car park, where the wind now rattles the masts of the yachts in the winter. Further on, through a gate, the grass was short and tufted and it became increasingly marshy towards the end. Old rifle butts rose up from the flat water-meadow, as this was once a rifle-range, used by the local yeomanry from the time of the Boer War up until the Second

World War. With the sliding river and all its myriad fascinations on one side, and the secretive, varied terrains of the marsh, bordered by the stream and the wooded bank, on the other, it had plenty for a young imagination to play with. The last and largest of the butts, right at the end below the woods, where it became really boggy, was almost inaccessible, and very mysterious. Some of it remains today. You will hear the skippers on passing pleasure boats telling their passengers that the area is called 'The Ranges', but this is not true. No Totnesian has ever called it anything but 'Longmarsh.'

It now begins just beyond the car park past the triangular turning bay, created for the timber ships twenty years ago. In the early 1980s the marsh was raised up by having a lot of rubble dumped on it, so that the shooting butts have disappeared. Although I mourned these changes, and still, when I think of the place, instinctively see it as it was before they happened, the magic is yet to be found. An old oak tree just beside the walk shows the original ground level. The whole marsh is owned by the South Hams District Council, who promise to manage it in an environmentally sensitive way. Occasional events are held here in the summer, but generally it is left to itself.

I have heard this stretch of the River Dart, 'home reach', described as the least beautiful or interesting, but I cannot understand how anyone can think so. To me it is one of the loveliest and most romantic. Look at the hanging woods across the water, and see how, ahead of you, the river valley seems to open up into a broad lake, bright and inviting after the dark woods, with no obvious way out. In front, above the trees, is the ruin of Windwhistle Cottage, and the river appears to go to the left, around Windwhistle Hill, but this is only a slight bend, because actually it flows sharply to the right, before going left almost immediately afterwards. You can see the tops of vessels going first one way and then the other above the low saltmarshes before vanishing, and when very young I used to love watching the paddle steamers approaching this way; you would see just the upper half, with mast and distinctive black and yellow funnel, changing direction with what seemed bizarre rapidity, before the whole thing appeared from around the hill. I still feel that if I look hard enough I'll see one coming towards me, but alas this is unlikely; I described the fate of the paddlers in *Boat Trip Down the Dart*...

When you reach the end of the path, where the stream comes out below the trees, sit and watch the river for a while, and take in its loveliness as it widens out and away, with the distant hills above the saltmarshes. Cormorants can be seen fishing, and there is one particular tree on the far bank where these strangely ancient looking birds like to sit and dry their wings; look also for herons, shelduck and Canada geese, and of course listen for the woodpecker on the hill opposite.

When you are ready to go you can return by the path, or turn left past the old sluice gate. Here are the remains of the shooting butt, and you can see some of the original marsh. A new path takes you right around by the stream, or you can walk across the raised area, now settling down and colonised by buddleia, willow and a host of other shrubs, flowers and grasses.

Back at the turning bay you get a good view of the town up ahead. J.M.W. Turner painted the scene from somewhere around here in 1824, but the result is not exactly an accurate topographical representation. This was a time when the English landscape had to resemble that of classical Italy, so he made the cliffs on the left of mountainous height, with the town spread over some distant, heavily wooded hills. The castle is several times too large, and the church is white instead of red; Totnes is transformed by Turner's expansive, ennobling vision into an

ancient dream-city across the water. This simple walk, even on the dullest days, always has a similar expansive, and perhaps ennobling, effect. If the cafe is open on Steamer Quay, stop and have a coffee and absorb for a while longer the endlessly changing life of the river.

— WALK SIX —
TOTNES DOWN HILL TO FISHCHEATER'S LANE

A ferny ramble through past and present. Approx. two miles, taking about an hour and a half, but you can easily make an afternoon of it.

From the Tourist Information Centre turn right, and follow the road around by the Job Centre, then turn left opposite the *Totnes Times* office into Warland. This pleasantly old-fashioned street was once on the waterfront, the whole area between the main street of the town and the southern hills being originally a tidal creek, until the first dam was built along here in the thirteenth century. The reclaimed area was called 'weirland.' Just past the Home Meadow old peoples home go left up Moat Hill, and carry on when it turns right at the entrance to Sharpham Drive. Notice the lovely old walls on both sides. At the next junction,

by Cherry Cross, go left and keep on up Totnes Down Hill. Take your time, and don't forget to keep looking back at the vista below, as it opens out until you can see for many miles across the countryside. This has always been one of my favourite walks, and I never tire of the sight of the town and river in their gentle setting beneath me. But giving close attention to the minutiae of life in the banks and hedges is equally satisfying, and this walk is particularly enjoyable for lovers of ferns, those most ancient and Devonian of plants.

In the 1870s a Totnesian called Francis George Heath published a delightful book, now long-forgotten, entitled *The Fern Paradise*, in which he described the lanes you are walking through, and the abundance of fern life to be found in them. I have not been able to discover very much about Heath, not even his dates of birth and death, but the impression I get from his book is of a sensitive, idealistic man living in London (Hackney, in fact) whose greatest joy is to revisit his native countryside in search of his beloved plants. With typical Victorian earnestness he clearly believes that the cultivation of ferns will bring spiritual, moral and social benefit to all who practice it, and the title refers both to the South Devon landscape and to the fern garden the reader can create in his or her own home. Heath's other works, all of which have sunk without trace, include *The Fern World*, *Burnham Beeches* and *The Romance of Peasant Life*.

He states confidently that 'No choicer spots for the lover of ferns can be found anywhere in Great Britain than in the neighbourhood of Totnes.' His evocations of the lanes are as luxuriant as the foliage itself, and he assures us that they were written *in situ*, 'under the sheltering canopy of over-arching trees and shrubs.' Lane romantics following his route today will find little changed, while the ferns, descended, I am told, from the rootstock of the plants he would have seen, grow as abundantly as they did over a hundred years ago. For me, his writings add an extra dimension to the experience of this walk. Because, I suppose, walking in these out-of-the-way, sunken pathways is such a private pleasure, best enjoyed alone or with a kindred spirit, a natural affinity is felt with anyone else who, also alone, discovered the same joys here in other times: a shared secret.

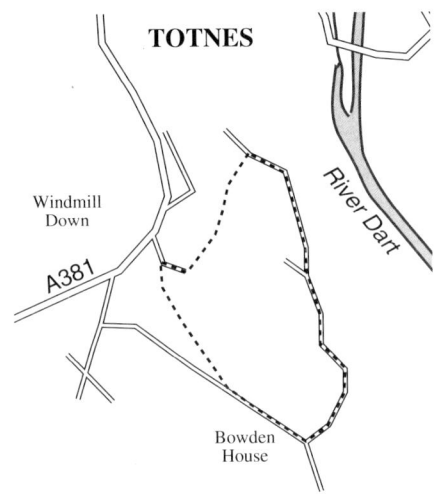

In the hedgebank on the right going up the hill Heath found, as you can, hartstongue, male fern, broad buckler and soft prickly shield fern, as well as, of course, great numbers of spring and summer flowers.

'Arrived at the top of the hill,' he writes, 'we have in front a park gate, leading to somebody's mansion, and two turnings for choice, one directly to the right, the other directly to the left. Both are charming, but the one to the right is irresistible. The left turning is a road; the right one is a lane. No fern hunter who might reach this turning-point when out for a saunter, would hesitate for one moment.'

Don't hesitate then, but step into the lane, enjoying its peacefulness and timeless quality, and its riches of sheltered plant life. After a while another lane appears, branching off to the right for a little way and then going sharp left. Heath, when he reached this point, became positively rapturous, and, seeing exactly what he saw, so long ago, you can understand why: 'A lane within a lane ... like a summer bower.' The new lane, running down the hill, is 'the most beautiful green and ferny lane which it is possible for the imagination to conceive...' a 'glorious wealth of waving green, wild flowers and fern-fronds...' There is, indeed, something special about this secretive, high-up, fecund place on a still, summer day, when all is quiet. 'As far as we can see, it appears to melt away in shadowy green, as it sinks down over the declivity of the hill.' Walk softly into it, as he did, and be embraced by its magic.

Occasional gaps, on the way down, give you magnificent views of the distant countryside and of Totnes 'which, nestling around its tall church tower, appears to repose in the very depth of the valley.' At one place you will have to go through a couple of gates, where two fields meet across the path. This lane, and the one it branches away from, was neglected and sometimes impassable for many years, but now the Devon County Council has officially classified them both as rights of way, and made them free of obstruction. Had you continued along the first lane it would have brought you, after clambering down between mossy banks, through leaf-mould and the debris of trees felled by the 1990 storms, to the road for Ashprington and Tuckenhay.

Eventually you reach the bottom, and meet yet another lane coming down the opposite slope and going off to the right. A stream from the left also joins it at this point. This is Fishcheater's (or Fishchowter's) Lane, to my mind the most romantic of all those around Totnes, the one I would most like to live next to, and be able to walk into from my house at any moment. It starts by the old toll house on the main Dartmouth to Kingsbridge road, now high above you. Turn right into Fishcheater's, which is narrow, dense with foliage, bright green and damp. Heath, in his sensual description of it, almost anticipates D.H. Lawrence; whoever said the Victorians were repressed? The name is said to derive from the time when tolls had to be paid to land goods at the quays in Totnes, so the fishmongers would disembark further down the river and slip up the lane, thus avoiding the charges. Notice a covered reservoir on the right.

Towards the end, as the old roofs of Totnes appear before you, three atmospheric figures carved from wood, and now quite weathered, stand on the right, where some steps climb the hillside: a man, woman and child. They were made and left here many years ago by a sculptor called Douglas Rous, who also created a madonna for the churchyard at Staverton.

This loveliest of green walks now finishes as you come out onto Maudlin Road. A right turn quickly brings you to Cherry Cross; go left down the hill and you are soon back in the town centre.

— WALK SEVEN —
THROUGH BRIDGETOWN TO FLEET MILL AND LONGCOMBE

A challenging walk up and down the red-soil hills, but very rewarding. Be prepared to get muddy. Approx. five miles, taking at least two and a half hours.

From the Plains cross over the bridge and go right, but at the turning to Steamer Quay and the Longmarsh go straight ahead, into the pleasant suburbs of

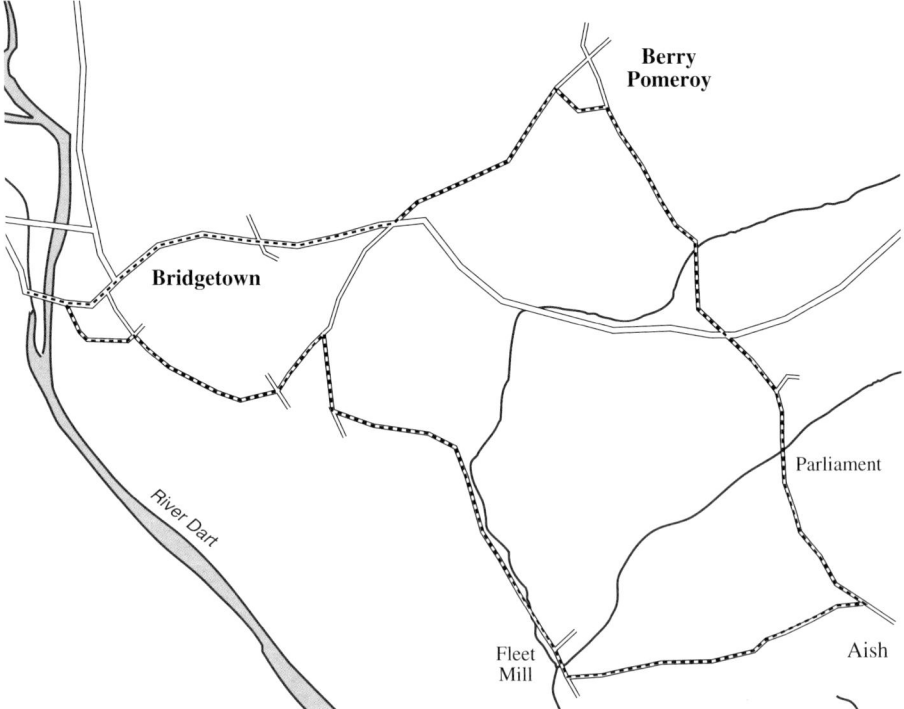

Bridgetown. Keep on until you reach the Primary School, and turn right down the hill. At the bottom go left, into Weston Lane, which climbs steeply up between the neat bungalows with their tidy gardens. Stop at the top to look back at another wonderful view of Totnes and the countryside rolling away to the moors, then go straight on, over the brow of the hill and into a rocky sided, muddy country road. On the right is a green lane that leads over the hills towards Windwhistle, with some good long views of the town, and then comes to a sudden end at the bottom of a field, so don't take it on this occasion, but go on past the farm and turn right when you get to the entrance for Weston House. Go up the lane for a little way, then turn left into a narrow lane that immediately goes steeply downwards.

This lane, about which I have written in both *Boat Trip Down the Dart* and *The Ghosts of Totnes*, has always rather haunted me. It is very rocky and always wet, but the sense of going deep into the ancient landscape is very satisfying, with the high, fern-covered banks and the richly coloured hills closing around you. I have a stronger feeling of the reality of past ages in many of these old lanes than I do at most historical sites. It is hard to believe that you are so close to the houses and bungalows of Bridgetown, so hidden away have you become from anything conspicuously twentieth century.

At last the path reaches the bottom of the valley and goes around to the right. Apart from the sheep moving on the hillsides above, you will probably be completely alone, and the only sound is likely to be the stream flowing energetically beside you. Walk on through the landscape, letting yourself become completely absorbed in the mysterious quality of the place, moving ever more deeply into it. Whenever I think of the experience of walking this lane I am reminded of music, something very English, modal, earthed yet with a contemplative, mystical quality, by someone like Vaughan Williams, Holst or Ireland. The walk feels as much an inner as an outer journey; the elements around you, the narrow path, mountainous hills, woods and stream, are all richly symbolic, as in an old folk-tale. But don't become too lost in the fantasy, because along here you are almost certainly going to encounter some mud, and there is nothing symbolic about it. Don't let it stop you, though, just plunge on, and you'll be amazed at how exhilarating it can feel!

After the worst of the mud you find yourself approaching the lovely old farm of Fleet Mill, always a surprise in this place seemingly so remote and inaccessible, and again like a cottage in an old tale. There is a road around to the left, which explains how the people who live here get to it, but go straight on, noticing the expanse of saltmarsh below the hill on the right. In August and September this is bright purple. A path ahead of you skirts the marsh and if you go along it you eventually come out at Fleet Mill Quay on the River Dart, where the remains of an old paddle steamer lie against the wall. Our route however veers to the left, and starts climbing upwards. This is a really archetypal Devon lane, narrow, rocky, dense with ferns and mosses, warm, always bright green, even in the winter. For much of the year it also doubles as a stream.

It seems to go on for ever, but in the end you reach a plateau and it opens out, with wide views towards the river and Stoke Gabriel. Usually it is all very still and peaceful. After a while you come to a proper road again, near Aish, and turn left. Now you can see the country which you have been inside, with its curving hills, the bright pink of the ploughed fields, the emerald green of the grass, the small copses and clumps of trees.

The road plunges down and up again towards the main Totnes to Paignton road. On the left you pass the attractive old thatched house known as Parliament Cottage, where tradition has it that William of Orange stopped for a meeting with supporters in 1688 on his way from Brixham to Exeter. An old stone in front of it is inscribed with the story.

Crossing the main road, go through the gap past the cottages and down, then turn right along another narrow, hilly road towards Berry Pomeroy. Don't miss the little bridges over the stream in the fields on both sides. From the top of the

rise, the road runs down beneath some ancient trees to the village, past a pond and the ivy-covered ruin of a medieval tithe-barn, then left, beside the manor house and the church: a perfect English scene, all green and grey, with the gentle grumbling of pigeons from the churchyard trees. If Berry Pomeroy had a pub, it would be good to stop for a drink, but in a place like this it would probably be a very up-market eating house, and I fear they would look askance at anyone who showed signs of such intimate contact with the countryside as you are likely to reveal!

From Berry Pomeroy take the road to Totnes, which joins the busy Paignton road at True Street. From here the roar of traffic accompanies you into town; a shame, but your mind should be full of images and impressions from the walk, reminders that noise and confusion are not the only realities, and perhaps you will find that it has had a deeper, more creative effect than you expected.

AFTERWORD

These seven walks around Totnes are, of course, far from being the only ones worth doing. Infinite variations are possible, and just following a couple of routes would have shown you other potential walks along footpaths, lanes and country roads you didn't take, but which are there, waiting to be explored. Wherever you are in Totnes the green horizon is visible, inviting you away from traffic and noise to the fields and hedges with all their myriad forms of life and their memories of past times. Unlike the epic long-distance paths across the moors or along the coast, walks in the Totnes countryside need no specialist equipment or skills, and little preparation – you can just walk off in any direction and soon be alone in the gentle, fertile landscape. I hope this book has encouraged you to do that, and trust that you will have found, and continue to find, endless pleasure and inspiration, even, this being Totnes, increased wholeness and wellbeing, in so doing.